! A.M.

Bottes du Roses

To Nextic from Miztli

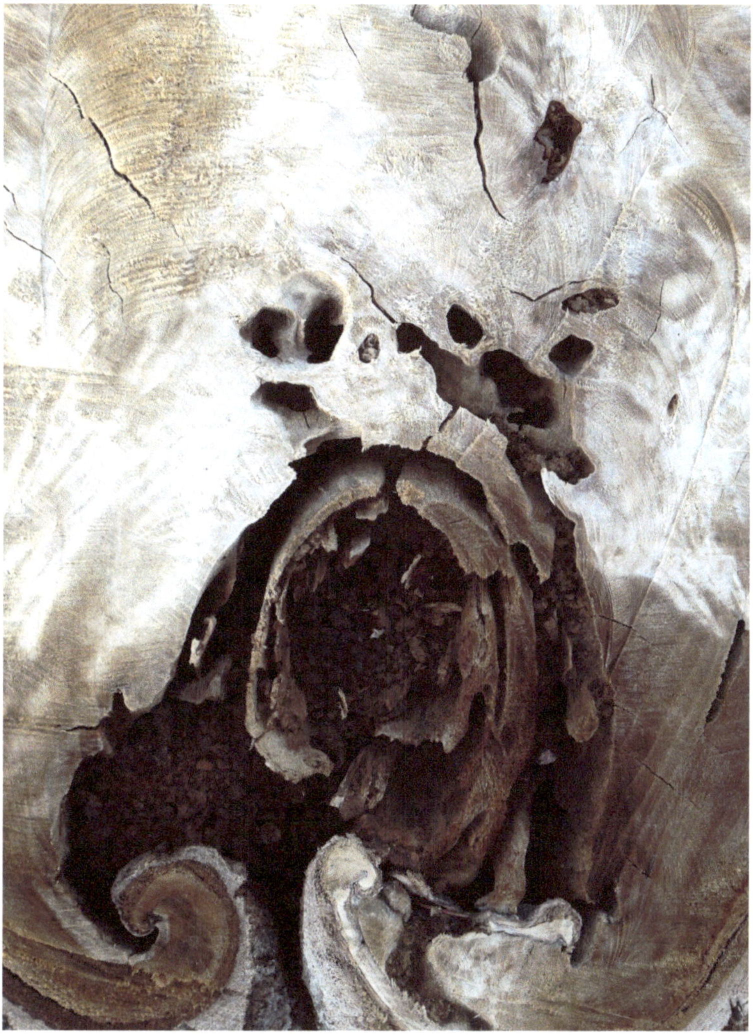

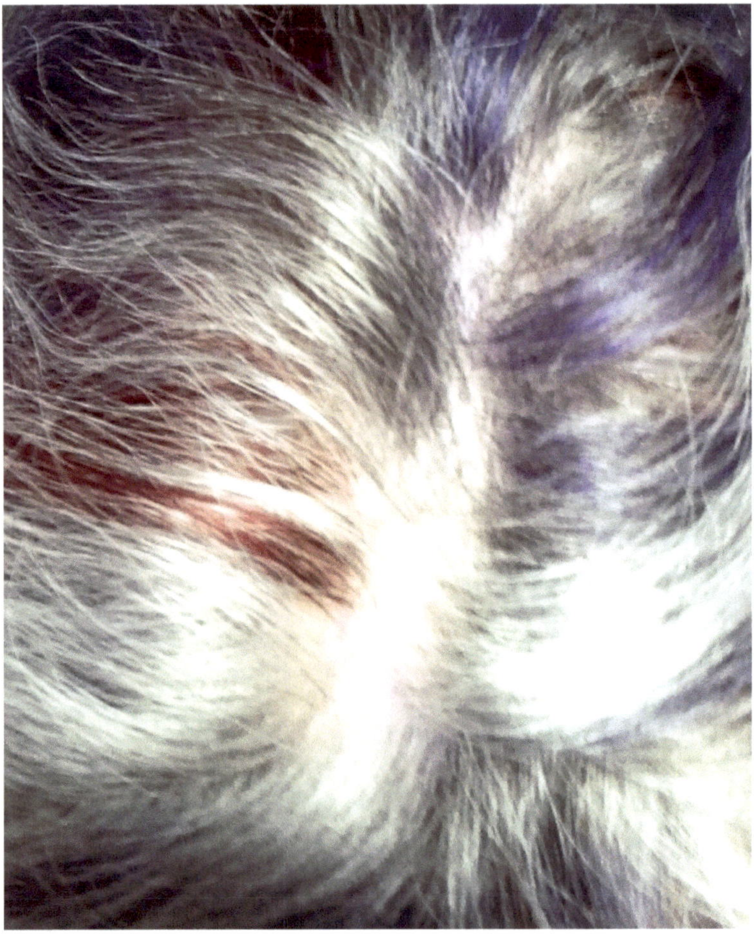

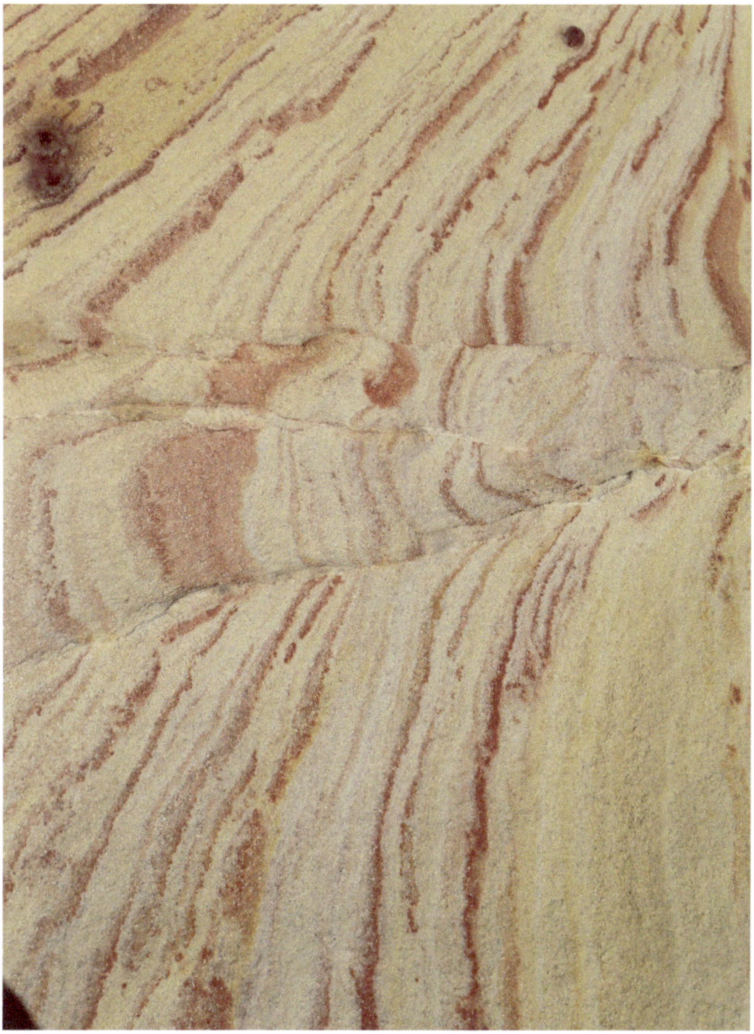

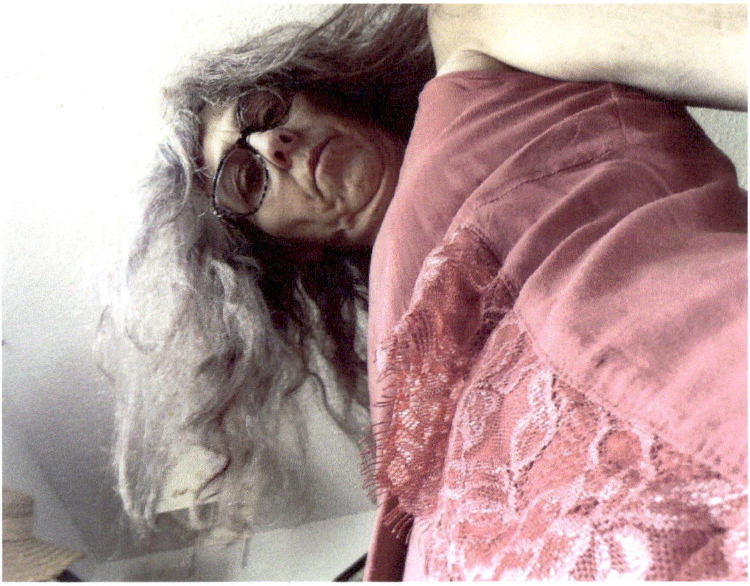

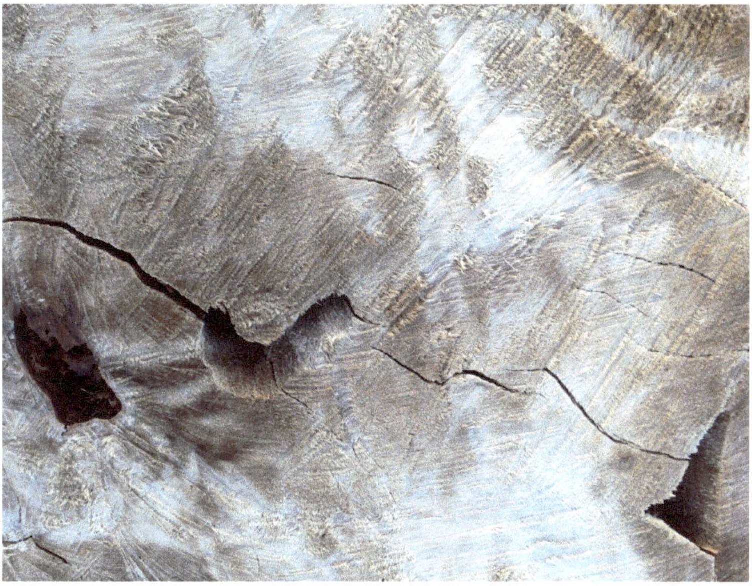

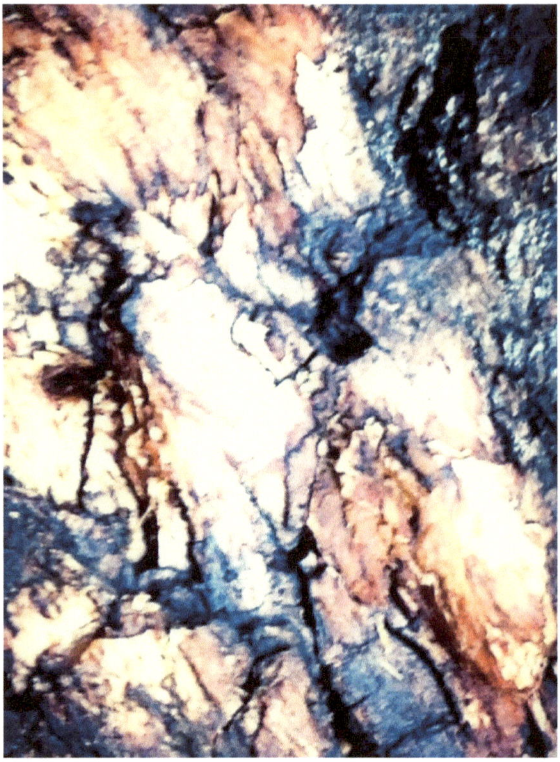

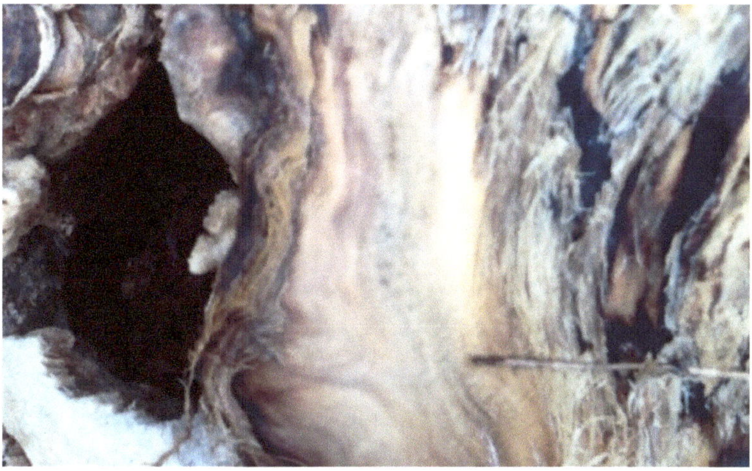

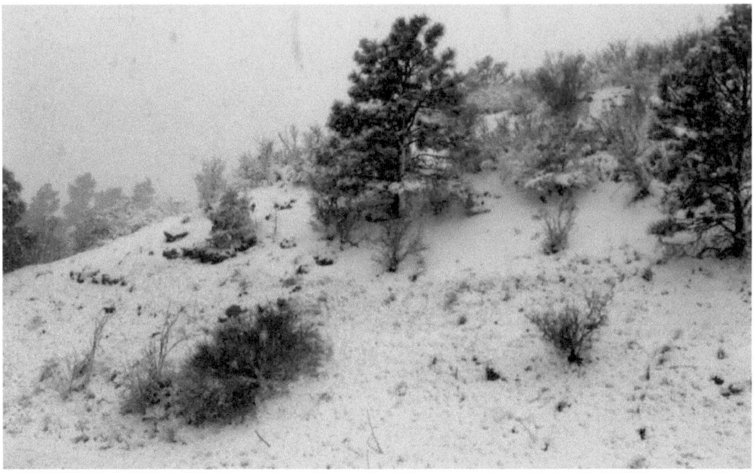

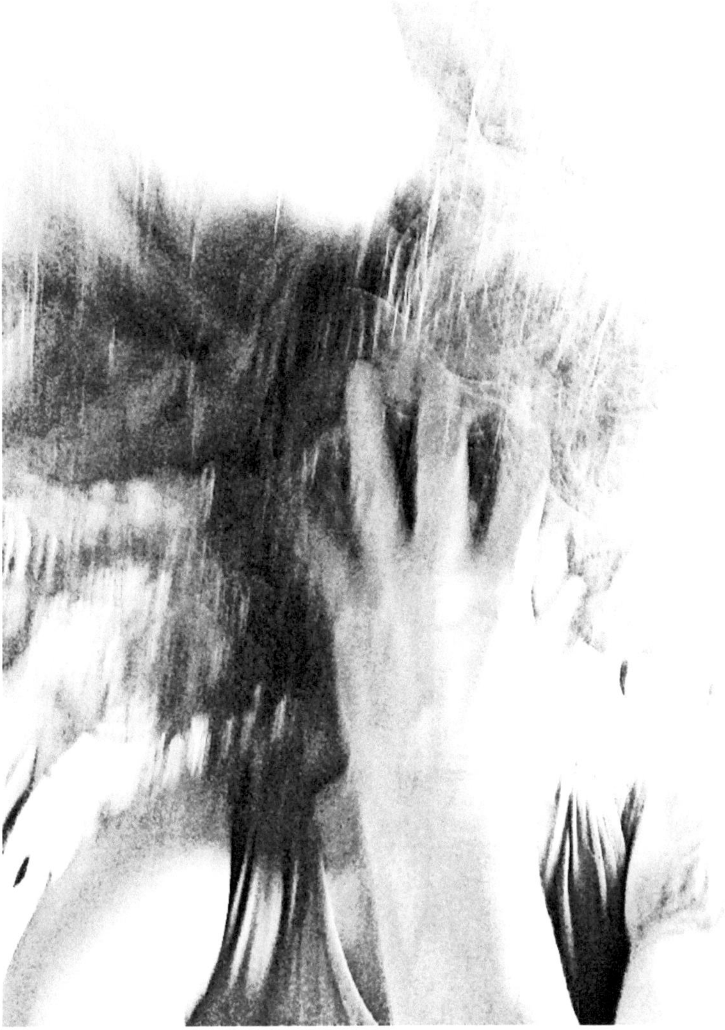

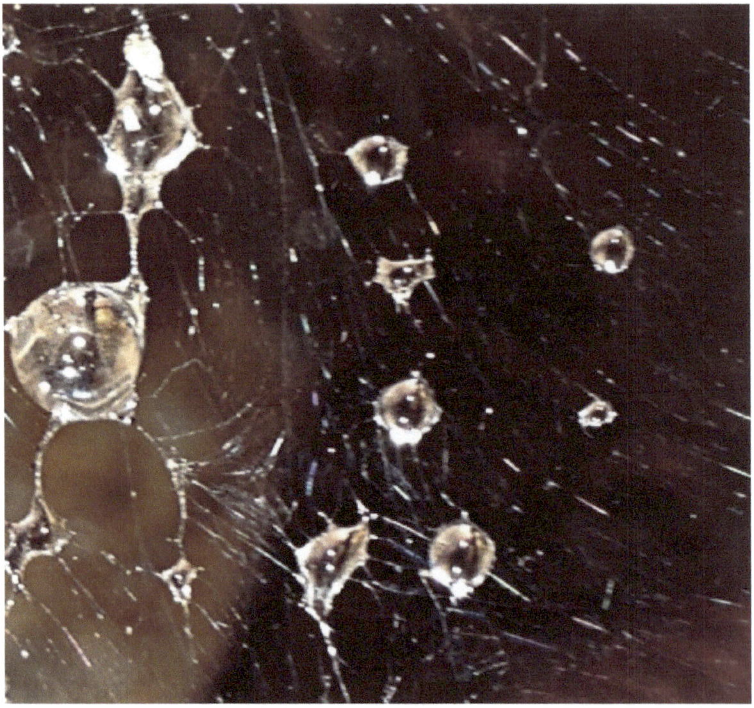

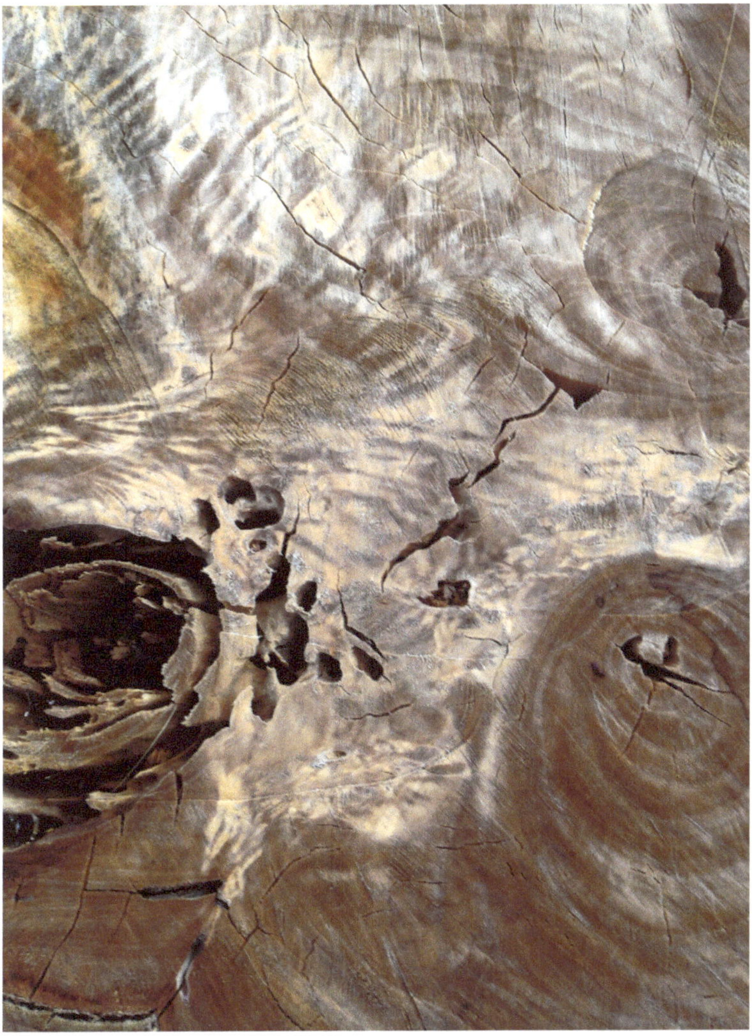

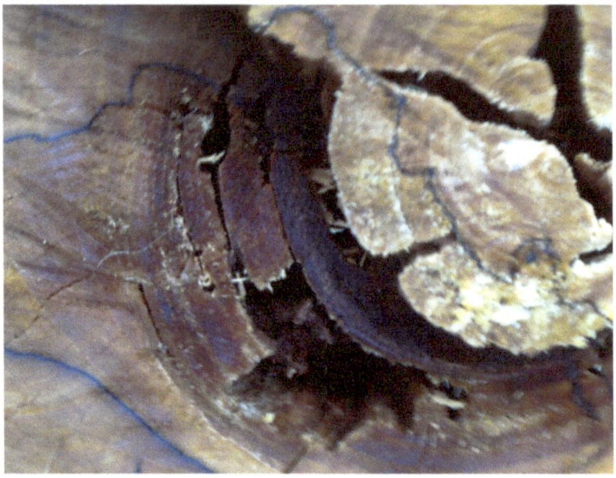

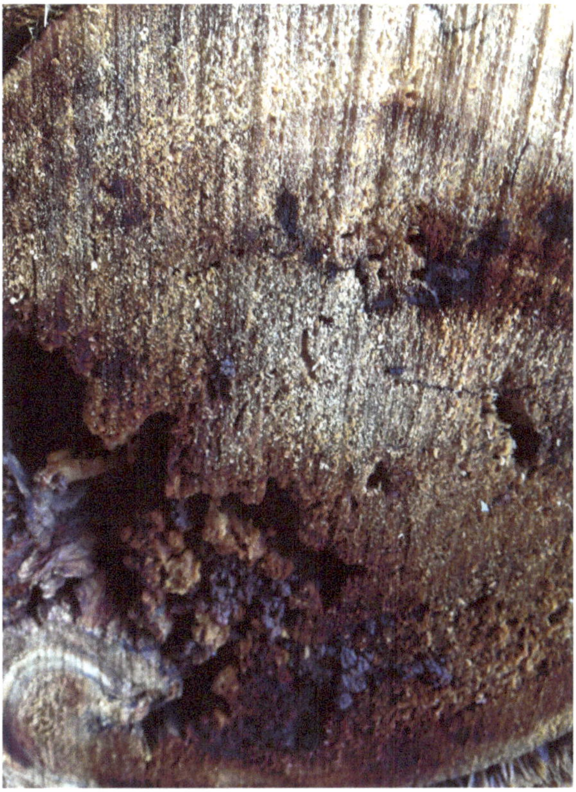

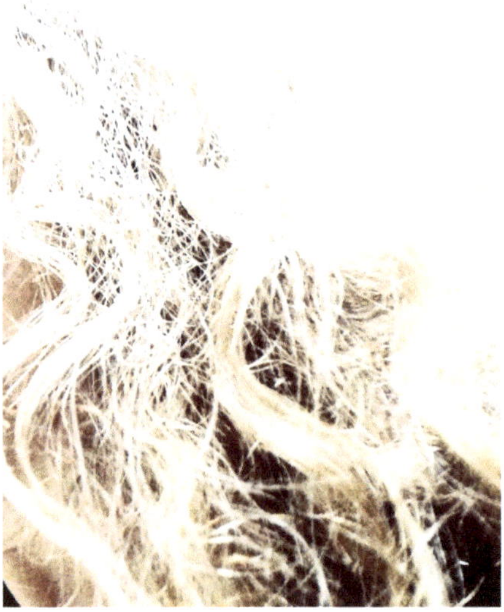

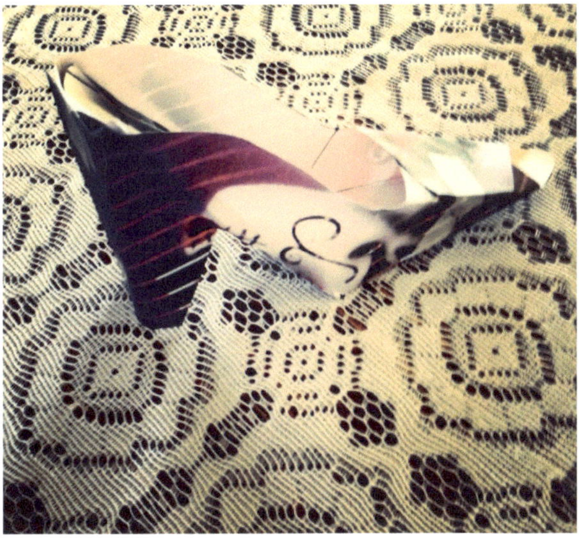

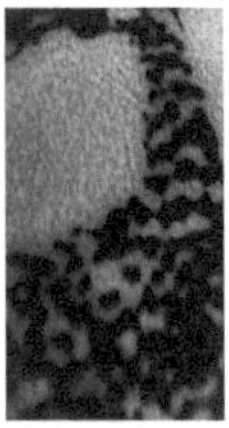

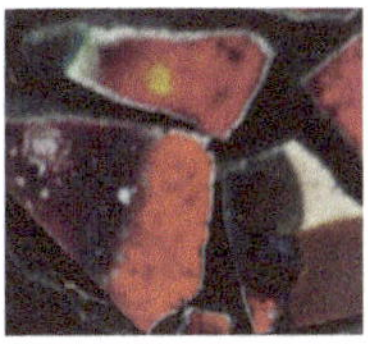

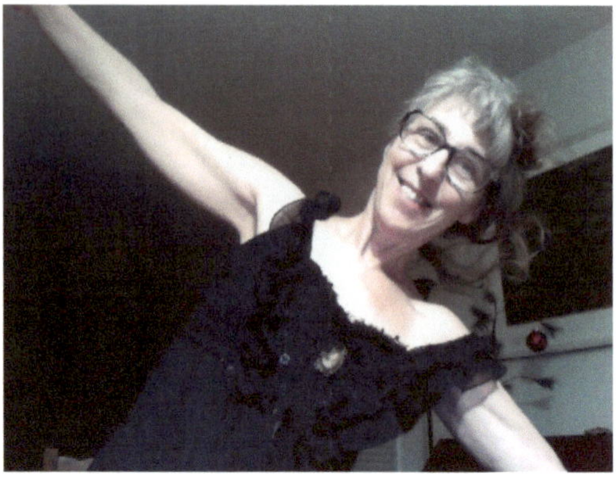

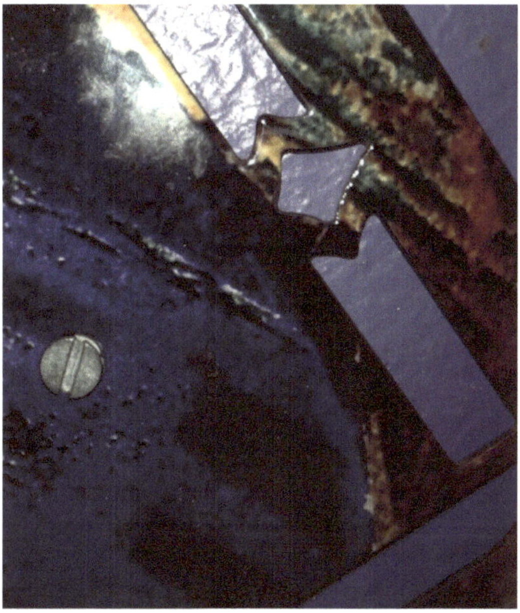

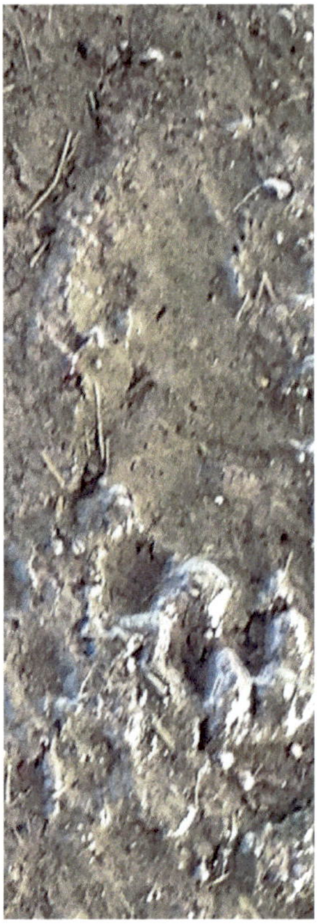

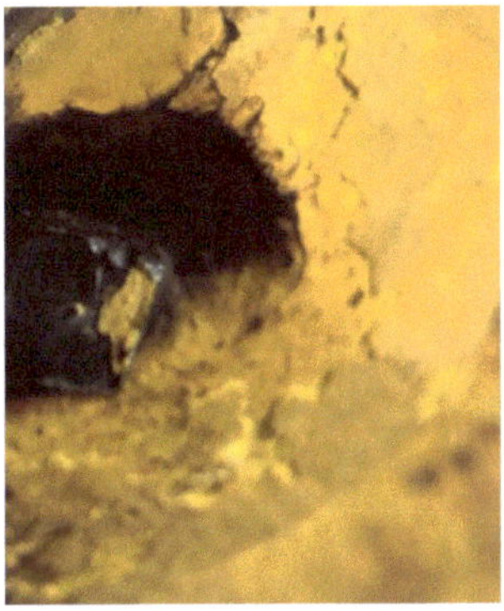

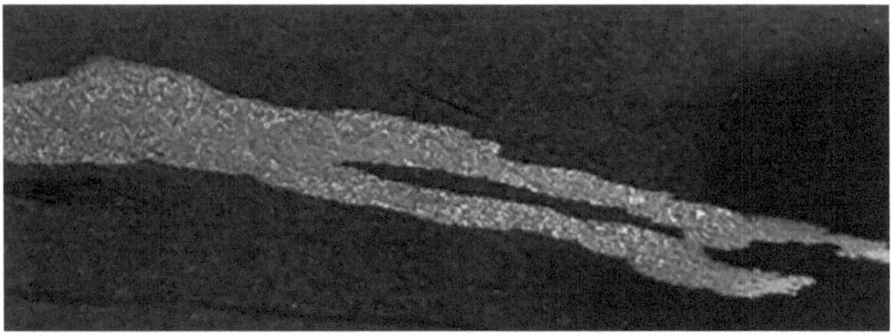

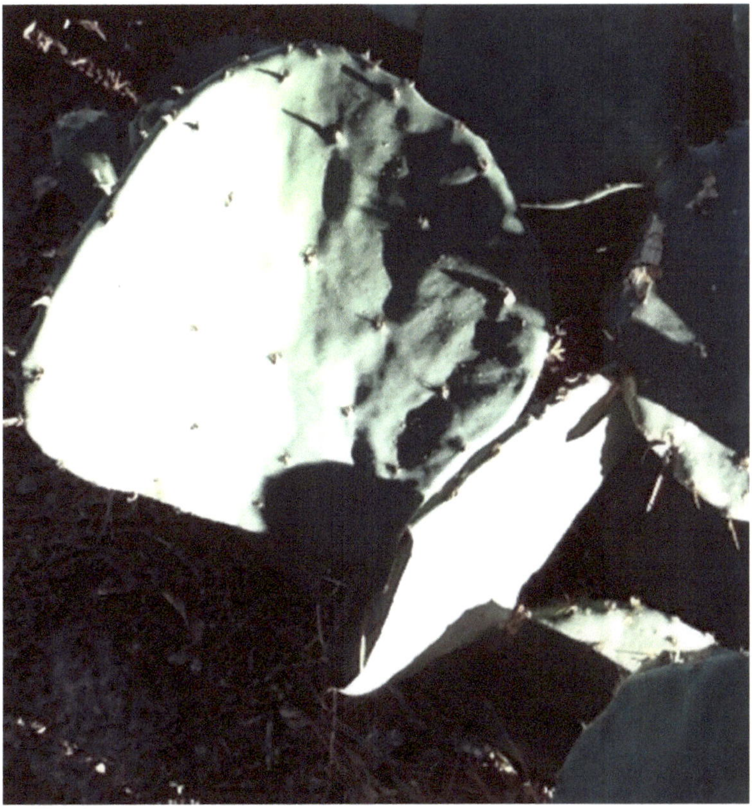

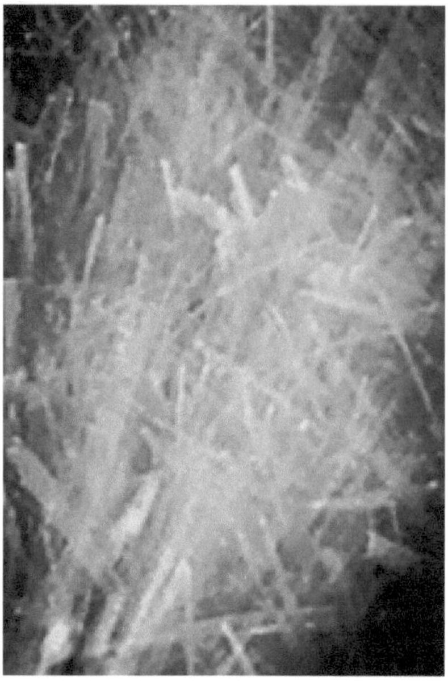

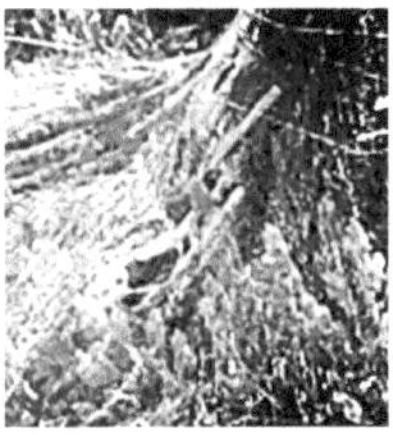

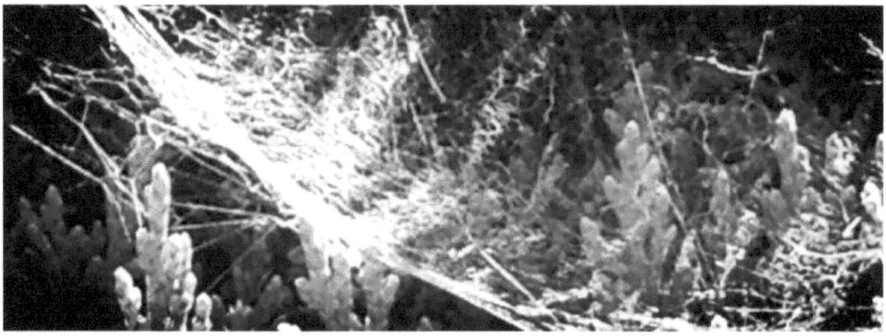

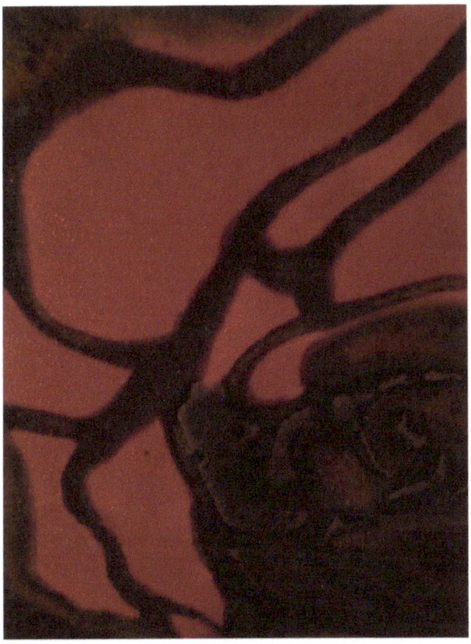

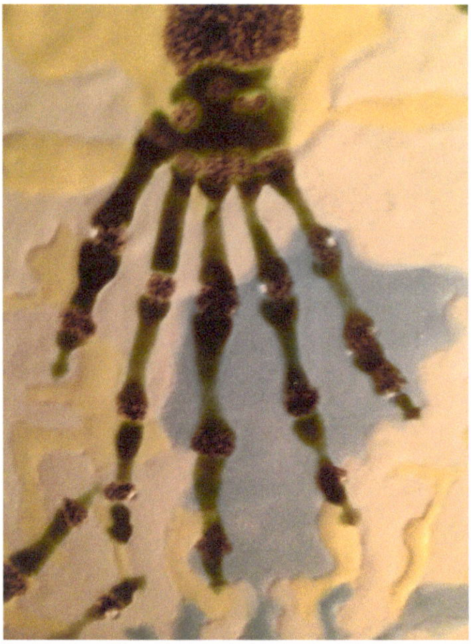

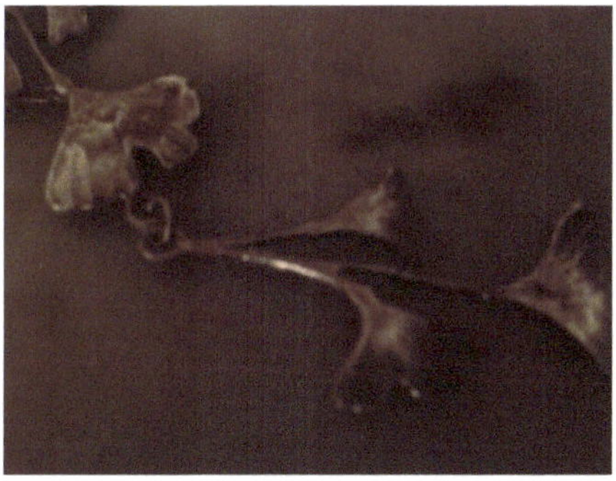

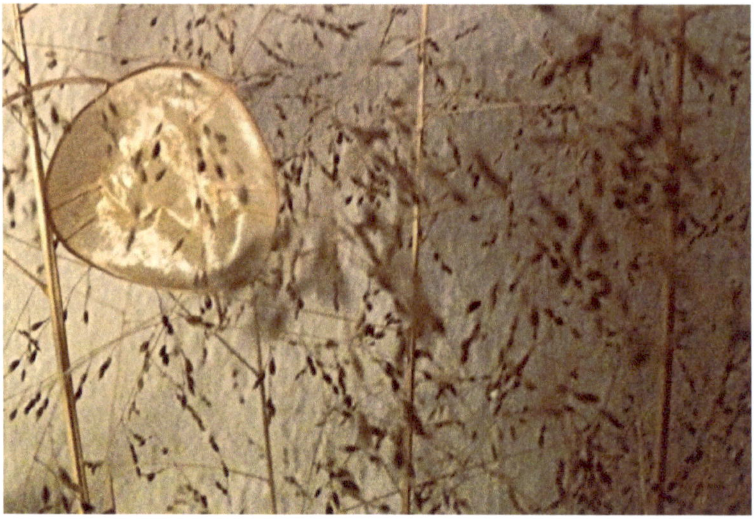

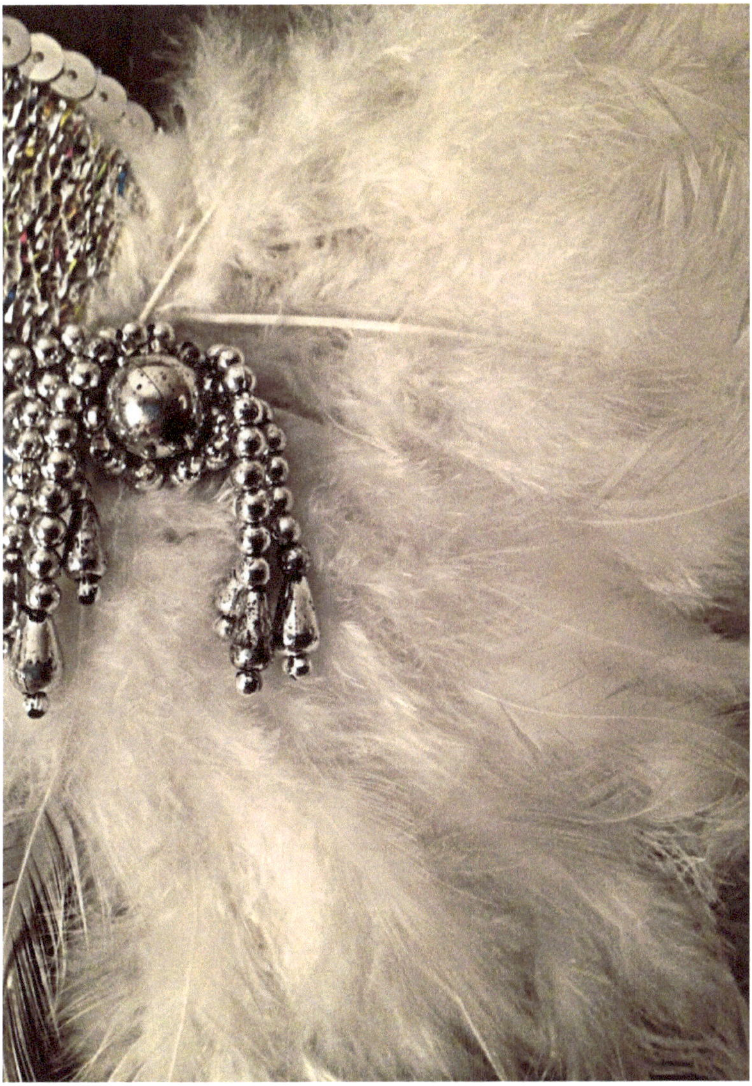

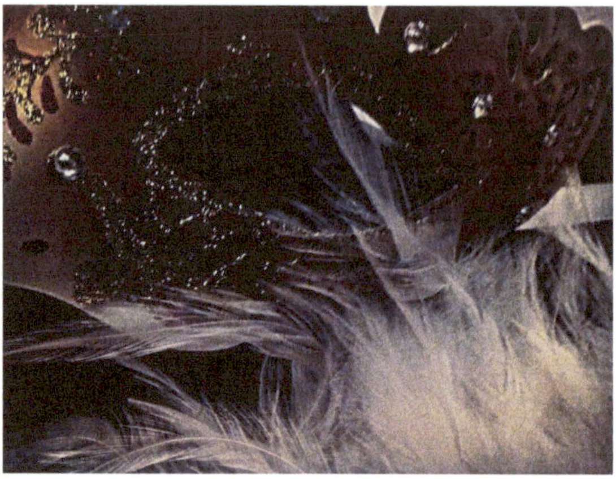

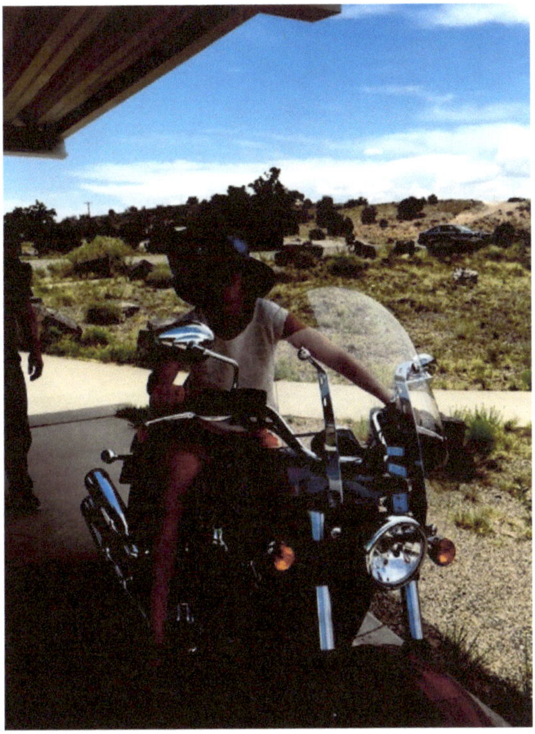

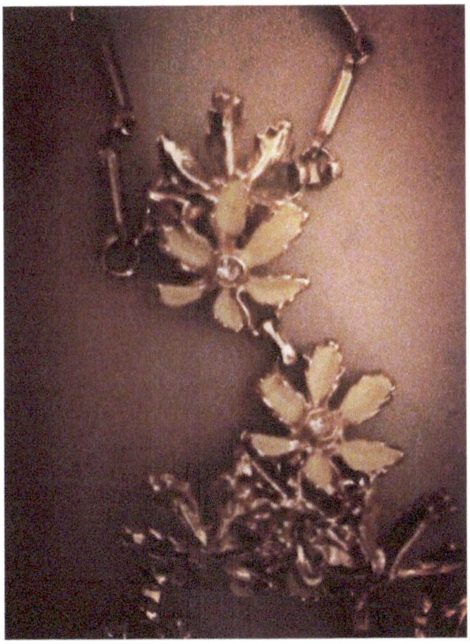

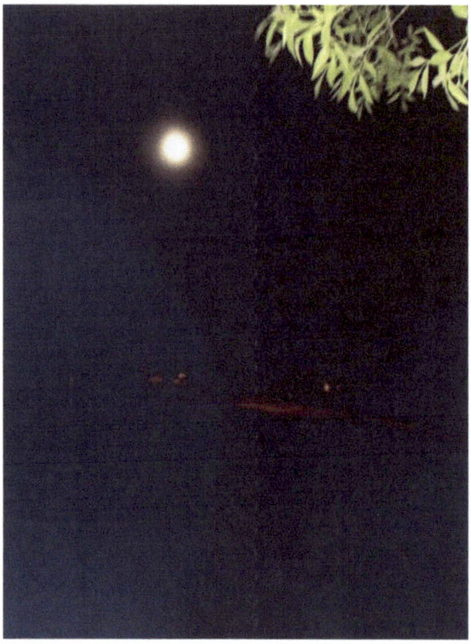

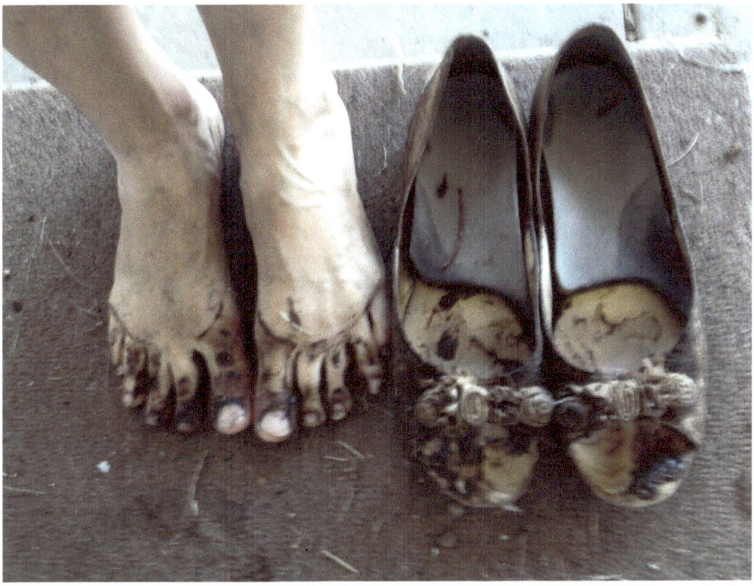

www.ingramcontent.com/pod-product-compliance
Lightning Source LLC
Chambersburg PA
CBHW040930180526
45159CB00002BA/689
9781515083665